T0011802

Life Cycle of a Pea Plant

by Meg Gaertner

FOCUS READERS®

PIONEER

www.focusreaders.com

Focus Readers is distributed by North Star Editions:
sales@northstareditions.com | 888-417-0195

Produced for Focus Readers by Red Line Editorial.

Photographs ©: Shutterstock Images, cover, 1, 7 (sky), 8 (sky), 21; iStockphoto, 4, 7 (soil and plant), 8 (soil and plant), 11, 12, 15, 18; Jean-Michel Labat/Science Source, 17

Library of Congress Cataloging-in-Publication Data
Names: Gaertner, Meg, author.
Title: Life cycle of a pea plant / by Meg Gaertner.
Description: Lake Elmo, MN : Focus Readers, [2022] | Series: Life
   cycles | Includes index. | Audience: Grades 2-3
Identifiers: LCCN 2021005882 (print) | LCCN 2021005883 (ebook) | ISBN
   9781644938294 (hardcover) | ISBN 9781644938751 (paperback) | ISBN
   9781644939215 (ebook) | ISBN 9781644939659 (pdf)
Subjects: LCSH: Peas--Life cycles--Juvenile literature.
Classification: LCC QK495.L52 G25 2022 (print) | LCC QK495.L52 (ebook) |
   DDC 583/.74--dc23
LC record available at https://lccn.loc.gov/2021005882
LC ebook record available at https://lccn.loc.gov/2021005883

Printed in the United States of America
Mankato, MN
082021

About the Author

Meg Gaertner enjoys reading, writing, dancing, and being outside. She lives in Minnesota.

Table of Contents

Chapter 1

Seed

A pea seed is in soil. The weather turns warm. Rain makes the ground wet. The seed is ready to grow.

The seed opens. A tiny **root** grows down into the ground. It holds the plant in place. A small **shoot** grows up to the surface. The shoot reaches sunlight.

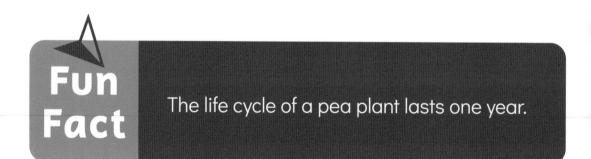

Fun Fact

The life cycle of a pea plant lasts one year.

Chapter 2

Seedling

The root takes in **nutrients** from the soil. These nutrients help the plant grow. The root also takes in water.

The seedling has tiny leaves. These leaves take in a gas from the air. They also take in sunlight. Leaves use the sunlight's energy. They turn the gas and water into food. Plants use the food to grow.

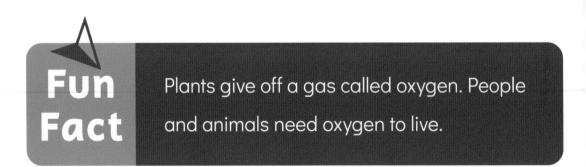

Fun Fact Plants give off a gas called oxygen. People and animals need oxygen to live.

Chapter 3

Flowering Plant

The pea plant grows. Its **stems** get longer. They might grab on to nearby objects. They climb up fences or posts. The plant grows taller.

Underground, the roots keep growing. They take in more nutrients. Soon the plant grows flowers. These flowers can be colorful. Once the plant has flowers, it can make its own seeds.

Parts of a Flower

Flowers have two key parts. **Stamens** are long and thin. Their tips are sticky. They are covered in **pollen**. This powder has half of what a plant needs to make seeds. The **pistil** has the other half. A pistil has tiny bits deep inside it. These bits can become seeds. A pistil also has a sticky end.

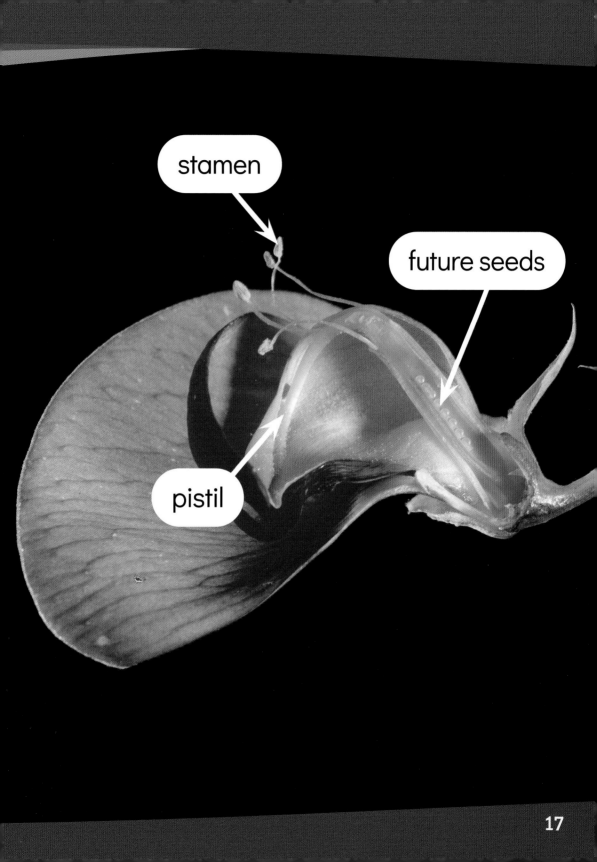

Chapter 4

Pea Pod

The pollen leaves the stamens. It reaches the pistil. It **fertilizes** the tiny bits inside the pistil. Those bits grow into seeds. The seeds form inside pods.

Over time, the pods dry out.
They split open. The seeds fall to
the ground. They reach the soil.
The life cycle begins again.

Fun Fact

Sometimes farmers collect pods before
they dry out. They remove the seeds. Those
seeds are the peas that people eat.

Life Cycle Stages

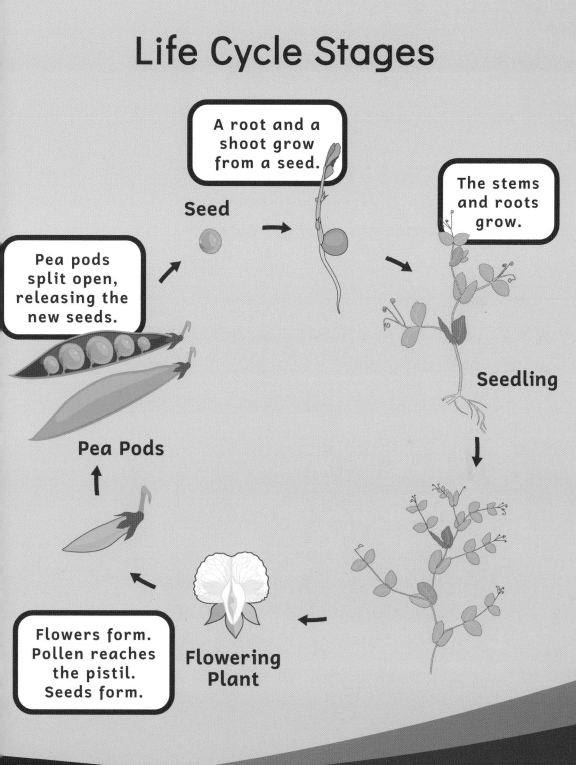

A root and a shoot grow from a seed.

Seed

The stems and roots grow.

Pea pods split open, releasing the new seeds.

Seedling

Pea Pods

Flowers form. Pollen reaches the pistil. Seeds form.

Flowering Plant

FOCUS ON
Pea Plant
Life Cycles

Write your answers on a separate piece of paper.

1. Write a sentence describing how pea plants make food.

2. Which stage of the life cycle do you find most interesting? Why?

3. Which part of the plant helps it make food?
   - A. roots
   - B. leaves
   - C. stamens

4. What would happen if pollen from the stamen did not reach the pistil?
   - A. The plant would not grow new seeds.
   - B. The plant would not get any nutrients.
   - C. The plant would not get any sunlight.

Answer key on page 24.

Glossary

fertilizes
Makes something able to grow a new plant or animal.

nutrients
Things that people, animals, and plants need to stay healthy.

pistil
The female part of a flower. It contains tiny bits that can become seeds.

pollen
A powder from male parts of plants. It spreads to female parts of plants to make seeds.

root
The part of a plant that takes in nutrients and water from the soil and holds the plant in place.

shoot
The part of a plant that grows up toward the surface when a seed opens.

stamens
The male parts of flowers. These parts contain pollen.

stems
The main bodies of plants.

To Learn More

BOOKS

Dunn, Mary R. *A Bean's Life Cycle*. North Mankato, MN: Capstone Press, 2018.

Huddleston, Emma. *Planting a Seedling*. Lake Elmo, MN: Focus Readers, 2021.

NOTE TO EDUCATORS

Visit **www.focusreaders.com** to find lesson plans, activities, links, and other resources related to this title.

Index

Answer Key: 1. Answers will vary; **2.** Answers will vary; **3.** B; **4.** A